# Songs from
# the Summer Kitchen

*poems by*

# Dawn Terpstra

*Finishing Line Press*
Georgetown, Kentucky

# Songs from
the Summer Kitchen

Copyright © 2021 by Dawn Terpstra
ISBN 978-1-64662-618-2 First Edition
All rights reserved under International and Pan-American Copyright Conventions. No part of this book may be reproduced in any manner whatsoever without written permission from the publisher, except in the case of brief quotations embodied in critical articles and reviews.

## ACKNOWLEDGMENTS

The author wishes to thank the editors of the following journals and anthologies in which these poems first appeared, often in earlier forms:

*Backchannels Journal*: "Sheltering"
*Cathexis Northwest Press*: "Signal Fire"
*Conestoga Zen: An Anthology* (Conestoga Zen Press): "Bamboo Forest," "Kitchen Vigil"
*Eastern Iowa Review*: "Kitchen Vigil"
*Flying South*: "Thunder" (previously "Gentle Thunder")
*Lyrical Iowa*: "Mirror, Flughafen Frankfurt, After a Bombing," "Drinking Tea in San Francisco"
*Meat for Tea: The Valley Review*: "Maribel"
*Neologism*: "self-portrait underwater"
*Passengers Journal*: "Bamboo Forest"
*Raw Art Review*: "Songs from the Summer Kitchen"
*Remington Review*: "The weight of afternoon sun"
*San Pedro River Review*: "Leaving Tucson"
*Sunbeams*: "Grace"
*SWWIM*: "Sweet Dills"
*Telepoem Booth*: "Grace," "Kitchen Vigil," "Ruby's last dress"
*Third Wednesday*: "Vacancies"
*The Write Launch*: "Ruby's last dress," "Morningside at the Desert Casino"


Publisher: Leah Huete de Maines
Editor: Christen Kincaid
Cover Art: Ryan Williams
Author Photo: Ryan Towe
Cover Design: Elizabeth Maines McCleavy


Order online: www.finishinglinepress.com
also available on amazon.com

Author inquiries and mail orders:
Finishing Line Press
PO Box 1626
Georgetown, Kentucky 40324
USA

# Table of Contents

I. **Plumeria breezes**
   Songs from the summer kitchen ..................................................... 1
   Ruby's last dress ............................................................................ 2
   River Dance in Botswana ............................................................... 3
   Savanna Sage ................................................................................. 4
   Grace ............................................................................................. 5
   Violet Waits at Base Camp ............................................................ 6
   Bamboo Forest .............................................................................. 7
   Maribel .......................................................................................... 8
   Invisible Robot Dog ...................................................................... 9

II. **Wonder after wait**
   Toward Memory .......................................................................... 10
   Return to Arch Cape .................................................................... 12
   Morning on Orcas Island ............................................................. 14
   Signal Fires .................................................................................. 15
   misaligned ................................................................................... 16
   Vacancies ..................................................................................... 17
   Leaving Tucson ............................................................................ 18
   Morningside at the Desert Casino ............................................... 19
   Thunder ....................................................................................... 20
   The weight of afternoon sun ....................................................... 21
   Tides Without Ocean ................................................................... 22

III. **The order of things**
   Sisters of Mercy ........................................................................... 23
   Home from the Flood .................................................................. 25
   self-portrait underwater .............................................................. 27
   Kitchen Vigil ................................................................................ 29
   Drinking Tea in San Francisco .................................................... 30
   Mirror, Flughafen Frankfurt, After a Bombing ........................... 31
   Presence ....................................................................................... 32
   Sweet Dills ................................................................................... 33
   Sheltering .................................................................................... 34
   May Vining .................................................................................. 35

# *Plumeria breezes*

**Songs from the summer kitchen**

begin with nail polish and the smell of rubbing alcohol.
My Palauan sisters' dark hair swings soft across eyes,
knees up, rubbing My Paprika is Hotter than Yours from long toes.
We sing the gossip like plumeria breezes early in the morning.
Full-throated love calls join from bantams in the alleys
beneath the betel nut trees, behind the Island Grocery, everywhere
love might be, like those women smoking on the beach by the marina,
we want to know, who are they, too much boob, those whore earrings?
Rice pot purrs, promises of yellow fin and mango after rain.
Sister moves the Buddha head found in Mami's taro patch,
brings out the Fritos, the tuu, the peanut butter, the lemons.
It's time for a wedding. A child already, the aunties are happy.
But brothers take the money the way they always do,
wives with big tastes and kids in trouble off-island.
We wrap slippery-slim tapioca in wet banana leaves.
My sister's husband says he fishes all day, but there are rumors.
By the light in the summer kitchen we watch him slide
snapper and ahi and wahoo in a briny pile on concrete after dark.
Our fingers make disemboweling an art for dogs to eat.
And what happened to you sister, you good woman?
Drugs made that boy crazy. See, he didn't want to kill you.
Bad things happen sometimes.
Sisters, you know how it is:
sleeping face-to-face on the floor in the girls' room,
air conditioner rattling too loud for dreams,
you scream into your hands, put ointment in your eyes,
and choose a new polish when roosters crow.

*Plumeria breezes*

**Ruby's last dress**

is the color of desert flowers
after a late spring monsoon,
purple pops on barrel cactus,
pink prickly pears pleated across
cotton the color of damp sand.

On a bench she waits for him through
a hot afternoon, wind gritty across her face.
Cross-legged she sits through ember-ash twilight.
Night hawk screes low into pinon scrub.

What a miracle if bodies gliding down sidewalks
were fish swimming through currents,
where he in a shadowed shallow
grabs for her, flapping fins, beating
heart clenched in one hand.

In dreams, water runs downhill
disappears down a sandy arroyo,
blessed by something that is not God.
But a magician with a bottle of Milagro—
as if dresses, fish, and he who once loved her
were only a mirage dissolving on some horizon.

## River Dance in Botswana

They rush like flood waters
atop the burning sands
of the Bongwanake River.
Past the shade of mashatu
and ziziphus trees

elephants in cow-calf pairs
pool slow, forelegs swing.
Sand sprays, trunks snake
two feet down to silent current
dark-cold and divined

tusked heads bob
legs shift,
flanks move together
day-dancing
to a pied kingfisher's song.

While your eyes find mine
and miss night moon's stare
cradled by acacia boughs,
only you can see blind waters
slide beneath summer scald.

*Plumeria breezes*

**Savanna Sage**

Pungent-fresh in the corners of my pocket I crumble
leathery leaves named for each afternoon of hunger.

Over his shoulder the sun rides above stagnant water,
a Woodland Kingfisher crescendos from the baobab,

tiny impala stills in scrub. My guide doesn't talk
about small endings, but each night death slides

from trees, travels the roads near camp, leaves
fat tracks at the river crossing. He points to a pair

of eyes beneath cascading thorn scrub. A shadowed
leopard with scars on her thinning flank tenses. Near

head-high mounds of sage, and umbrella trees swarmed
by termite spires, paws rush the bank, pull at leaping hooves,

engulf in a final spring—spotted veil covers an elegant form.

*Plumeria breezes*

**Grace**

All around the bus stop
sun spreads early, thick
across rooftops. Her mother
behind, Grace, a thin-legged girl,

sits with a round smile
blooming yellow
on a weedy-grass strip.
Between cars wheeze-breezing

toward the city, a trickle
of the early shift shuffles stiff
toward next week's groceries.
Dandelions by the dozen

pop waxy beneath the girl's
small criss-crossed legs.
She picks the most yellow,
dusting gold across her chin.

Green heads pinched,
cotton-ball fluff
sprays in her breath,
scatters at her knee,

floats down the strip,
leaps into currents
of passing cars.
Sowed through her delight,

next year's blight
stills to beauty
somewhere unexpected
in acts by small handfuls.

.

## Violet Waits at Base Camp

as beautiful and delicate as the flower
for which she is named.
Pale and blushed, fair-haired
with a heart-shaped face,
amethyst eyes with wide smiles,
she squats on the stoop
outside Coffee for the People,
framed by the remnant rainbow
from the Summer of Love. She is patient.

Festooned flower child, she's bundled
for a trek in her striped serape,
and fuzzy white pajama bottoms
patterned with Batman, Robin, and
red KaPows. How cold it may be
where she goes. Superpowers will serve her.

She stages the mutts, handsome
in hand stitched harness. She waters
the cat, lowers him from the stroller,
smooths his fur, dingy-flat. She's not afraid.

Her companions prepare for hours,
young sherpas securing supplies,
mapping routes, charging phones.
Her boyfriend sits next to her,
guitar at his feet. They share a joint.

Expeditions take many forms, her heart
the bright center of his. He maps a trip
to touch the stars, he knocks her up.
They move south in a daze. The cat dies.
She buries him with orange poppies.

I think of her smile,
expedition rounding the first corner
ahead of the advancing avalanche.

## Bamboo Forest

Light-footed and hushed
we still as in a holy place

*Bamboo sings for us*
I say to my adopted sister
harp-voices rise in leaf-filtered ether
fairies swirl beyond the path

Sweet ginger flower intoxicates
pepper-leaf-wrapped betelnut
reddens our mouths, spit
swims between cheeks

We stop near mami's taro patch
knee-deep and foot-sucked
beneath pendulous breadfruit
*tuu* reach to us with yellowing hands

magic melts into our family's familiar
pours through pounded poi
through fish heads she's learned to pick clean
we laugh, rolling gelatinous eyes on our tongues

Palauan *biib* calls like a jungle ghost
singing for our ocean aunties, the giant clams
craned to the surface by foreign hands,
ancestor memories seep through her song

I teach her the words

We are divine and mortal
ocean and fire
taro and manroot
treetops and seaweed

Will she know to mourn
the deepening silence between us

## *Plumeria breezes*

**Maribel**

is my UberXpress, drives a black Camry. Her smile on a day damp-heavy like a cool compress. She's seen so much, mornings through midnights, up and down the serpentine streets of San Francisco, nearly 3,000 times.

She is an artist, painting with people, who bring sunshine, even those drunk sometimes. Her husband is happy now, her sister is happy only if Maribel doesn't work nights. After 30 years, scrubbing floors and toilets, ten hours a day, six days a week, no time off for kids.

She visits her sister in Las Vegas, town of too much sand and heat. Maribel loves this city of water and ocean breezes more. Her sister asks about the late-night shadowed people who come with much darkness and maybe knives. Maribel is ok, the people are ok, not too many bad people here in a shell game that feeds freedom.

She keeps a snapshot of a dark-haired cherub in white onesie and stretchy headband on her dashboard. Her daughter will be a nurse someday. She is a good girl, a married girl. Maribel drives for her. Her son is headed to college, he's always a good boy. Maribel drives for him. Maribel is from El Salvador.

She drops me off at the exhibit and there are photographs here Maribel should never see. A teenage boy, bound, blind-folded in a shared grave. Women stand nearby, searching through the carnage for the faces of loved ones. What pictures are painted upon her memory?

In single strokes, she cut the head from the serpent. Murderous memory dissolves to American dreams.

Maribel, I rate you five stars.

*Inspired by the SF MOMA exhibition "Meditations" by American photojournalist Susan Meiselas, and the woman who drove me there.*

## Invisible Robot Dog

His third-grade stories spill each day
on plain white paper
held with three shiny staples,
punch with the power of the
robot dog he sees in her,
far from goats and camels
in the Sudanese village
where he was born,
far from cardamom and cinnamon
in the yellow house in the blighted neighborhood
down the street where they speak French,
and far from stone-faced adults and kids.
His smile, wide as the city his teacher saves.
Her power is secret
coming from lasers
fired by rows of spacemen
in pipe-like articulated suits,
her skin covered in monster-proof
scales, sleek, shiny, sci-fi reptilian.
Her boots, taller than a building,
a dorsal fin on the hatch
of her spacecraft
tipped with instant death.
She fights King Kong, Dog Man, Godzilla,
secret agents, UFOs.
Vicious battles in pencil
where she saves the kids,
monsters lose, the kids win food,
earn a trophy, they are the best.
He knows
someone can save them all—
and the world—
simply by hugging,
listening, laughing.

# *Wonder after wait*

**Toward Memory**

The wait scratches
behind the door
of summer's sultry end.

It whispers into hair
tucked behind my ear
cries a little until

a quick sharp
breath of tear-choked air
stings the nostrils,

burns the lungs—
as I run to meet you
on a late afternoon

in a room framed by maple
dripping reds and shadows,
your thick kiss

doorway to stolen
heart-bursting days ahead.
It reminds me of settling

into a seat aboard the train
from Rome to Florence,
and my surprise

at the green country
rushing past a window,
where tree-lined meadows

*Wonder after wait*

were golden and splotched
with shade, pigs wallowed
in holes, mud-caked snouts,

men in tweed coats with dogs
walked the fencerows,
lost in their pipes and solitude

like men I knew back home.
But the wonder-after-wait
of a city shimmering in its own

light pierced my narrow imagination.
My pulse staggered at ancient
skies and stars inscribed

across Gothic ceilings,
the hands of lovers
pushing the bolts,

door to Ponte Vecchio,
swinging open to
embrace the future.

Now we are the wait,
mired in months, desire,
tickets in pockets, while daylight

slides into streetlights,
spins across our weeks,
a compass emblazoned with suns.

**Return to Arch Cape**

I took my first long walk
on the beach this morning,
finding the tidal pools again.

After two years,
the ebb and flow
of this place
still the same.

Legions of gulls
doze in clusters after
a feast of Dungeness crab,
sand fleas hop
between savaged claws.
Distant arches glow,
salty mist rises
in early light,
puffins float like bobbers
at the base.

I see my own tracks
and the footprints
of countless others,
yet see no living person
from rocky point to rocky point.

A man with long strides
ran here with his dog,
maybe a black lab or a boxer,
tongue flapping wildly.
A woman played with two kids
who kicked off their shoes,
running back and forth
like sandpipers
to the water's edge.

## Wonder after wait

'Heather loves Tabitha'
sinks into the sand,
striated sandal tracks
disappear side-by-side
as tide crawls the beach.
Perhaps a young man
and water nymph
in white gauze and sea grass
danced around a bonfire last night.
Clumps of seaweed
lay here and there,
toes run through every bit.

I lift a sand-caked shell
to my ear and marvel,
how empty we arrive
upon this beach,
how quickly we fill
so full of ocean.

## Morning on Orcas Island

across a bay
green-spined islands
sleep above sea-stained mist
we climb into cloud forests
after making love
early on a Sunday

steeped in pine-laced daybreak
spiced fog kisses
find our foreheads
like lips of a mother
inside a vaporous wrap

conifer-moss drips toward
old growth's stone feet
time melts in moments
upon our tongues
strings of spun sugar

fine morning crystals
fired by joy's breath
pulled pliable
thick-with-sweetness
memory lustrous
beyond the beautiful hours

**Signal Fire**

Afternoon slides like a sigh
down twilight's slope, into the smooth
pocket of evening. I catch a spark
and start a blaze for you.

I've started many fires during the years,
in a circle atop this land of prairie hills.
Valleys stay cool with shade-tree woodlots
spit-sputtering with speckled streams.

In this wild place, winds blow close and
footpaths remain dark and dense. Days lost
in wandering; the chase swallows you whole.
On a hill, this fire and I burn tall for you to see,

sparks pop your name upon night's velvet.
Come, let's sit tight upon a rock,
share wine with our faces warm, laugh
at such foolish spirits ripened with age.

Tonight, we seek a less arduous adventure—
more the shelter of an embrace. As
darkness grows bright with embers' glow,
stones lose the heat of remembering.

**misaligned**

I watch the song sparrow
build a nest in a bluebird box
a bluebird weave grasses
and pine needles inside hickory rot
my growing affection
for displacement rivals

words woven by this keyboard
fat chaos skeined
from quaking boughs, suck
of mud, the soft belly of our animal
loosed in long strokes across a page

for now we sing each other
from here

        from there

*Wonder after wait*

**Vacancies**

We long to know the emptiness. To stand
on tiptoe peeking through splits in boarded

windows, to pry open the tall blue Victorian
heavy with shutters. We stroll beneath the sagging

portico along the path toward a weedy garden,
reaching for the splintered back door opening to air.

What happened, the old busker with missing teeth
doesn't know. But the star on a pole behind the house

marked the bus station, first place he fell in love—
fine girl with cut-off jeans, rosebud lips, nose that

wrinkled when she laughed. What if we scoop memories
like tiny fledglings calling from the grass, warm them beneath

our shirts, restore their beating hearts, wait until they
remember to fly? Would fresh-love rise inside our chests,

woven with gold-brown eyes, transistor crackling James
Brown, Greyhounds growling into the street? One day,

won't memory come for us, watching stars from the garden
bench, closing the back door, finding this poem on a table?

**Leaving Tucson**

Rising above the runway I see you were only
an idea   a quarter mile of abandoned earth
below   a breeze struck brightly as a crystal goblet

How the light softens city-circling peaks
and crevices   melts malleable highs into euphoric
dreams   kisses parched lips with ephemeral

waters   Snow on mountains reminds me
the season to climb with you is a summer
afternoon   the season to fall is every day

after   One last time above the Tucson
Mountains I watch day drown pink-
capped   wound-bound   bleeding behind

stone sails   Dust spins   illuminated above
a fading mesa   a pick-up rushes ahead
someone waving inside   I see now

it's only rain   another trick of light

## Morningside at the Desert Casino

Travel is a roll of the dice.

Today I am waking to your palette
spreading beyond the road,
dawn-kissed among
the Rincon mountains.

A big sky floor filled in misty
slumber, percolating purples
nudge stony shoulders
to sweep light's ticking

hands across another day.
Your yawn opens wide
valleys of Sonoran splendor,
saguaro and sagebrush spread

like a slow spill washing night
shadows into daylit drains.
Blue wind waves high,
streams for wispy-skiffs.

As the People say,
one sunrise those inside
will feel the sacred seed
spill from Mother's burlap

and wrap their fingers
into mountain's sandy feet.
But for now, shrieking pineapple
sevens and spinning double cherries

cascade by quarters—
half pulls at the rabbit hunger.

*Wonder after wait*

**Thunder**

growls in low farewell,
like a distant horn

on a ship sailing slowly
through billowing headlands.

I see you jump, laughing
beneath the pruning shake

of a lilac branch as captive
drops tumble. Fragrant goblets

pour showers upon your head.
Sun-touched tears trickle past

time-trenched wrinkles,
those I love to trace.

In your blue eyes
I see it smiling—

wet kiss of spring.

*Wonder after wait*

**The weight of afternoon sun**

is greater than the decades you moved
atop these honeyed wooden boards,

less than the words, songs, dustlight
dancing spirals between currents,

indelible patterns bleach across oak,
bright and maple-shadowed in the spring

blaze-grazed mid-September until winter
light thaws time's remembered heat.

I curled next to you as afternoons
slid toward the window like a rug

pulled for shaking, coffee mugs,
file folders, deadline-tight hours

catch a breeze exhaled before falling.
I tuck at your feet as a last ray recedes

to shadow, touches where you linger,
always closest to the light.

**Tides Without Ocean**

Morning roils, light splashes hard
against pavers down Main Street.

A chime opens the bakery door
with a fresh-baked welcome. Plaid-shirted

woman buys potato bread to sell
with homegrown beets and cabbage

on Memorial Square. At Hillsdales,
white-haired men in ball caps pour

coffees, shoulder-tight talk brings
the good word. Like who's the black-haired

woman for a month at Frank's? Must be
a witch or a Democrat. There's a pillow,

cold for a month two blocks away
where a lover's head no longer rests.

Across town, teen-girl-tough flips her
ponytail, grabs a softball glove and cleats,

clenches keys. The Carlsons, married 50 years,
forget words to their favorite song but dance anyway.

A nurse in blue scrubs holds a man's wrinkled hand,
listens to a story one more time. Women with walkers

glide up a ramp to sew blankets for the homeless,
but not for the girl and her baby in a Ford

behind the 7-11. Hope drowns in the undertow
of everyday waters. On still nights we comb

sidewalks for treasure, or a survivor face down
in a dream. What is the gift at the end?

# *The order of things*

**Sisters of Mercy**

my number bobs down the hall
from room 320 on a current of mobile vitals
a body counted in pulses and breaths
on a Dynomap
saline and antibiotic flowing like a tributary
forced into a vein
was it medicated an hour ago
a morning ago
urine bag attached to a bed
what's the output tonight
light from the street beckons
as if an ear leaning to the black roll screen
where does it hurt
why are you here
silence the gift I did not ask for
pain the anchor in a world slowly
spinning like a small boat in a wooded cove
let loved things sail past
because they are loved
let my quiet spot among branches
float upon still water
let me sing in the dark
faraway and mournful
like a barred owl in the bluffs
a reminder that a heart still beats
attached and unseen
calling tonight as if someone will listen

\*


Sister, you are more than a body.
I know your name, see your head
Upon a sanitized pillow,

## *The order of things*

I hear nurses speak your number in the hallway.

Yours is the 20th room on the right,
The middle of rounds,
The call light that never turns on,
The help that never comes because
You never ask.

I hold your hand,
Stroke your hair,
Feel your forehead.
I find the ice machine down the hall,
Fill a Styrofoam cup,
Find a plastic spoon.

You will be alright.

Sing to me the song
Of blue-black trauma,
Alone in a darkened room,
Fear mixed with body parts
Swollen, immobile, unrecognizable,
Traffic noise from outside the window.

Inside your drug-hazed dreams,
it is my heart that will beat.
I will help you breathe easy,
Then crawl back inside
When a face you know
Darkens the doorway.

Hold tight as we float this river.

*The order of things*

**Home from the Flood**

The summer of your sickness
floodwaters rise to your door.
We float you north.

On a day after the rains
the chicken noodle soup
in the Styrofoam carton
I carry from Perkins pick-up
is warm when you cup
your hands around it, holding it close
like coffee in a bone-brittle cold.

You crush crackers in cellophane,
slurp from a plastic spoon,
noodles bob like flotsam in the broth.
We watch Lawrence Welk,
a tenor sings Shenandoah,
you smile wide, mouth the words
like a forgotten name,
*look away you rollin' river.*

Outside a brick bungalow
broken concrete on the stoop,
pots of leggy lobelia and marigolds
droop their heads to the door.
Inside a room with green walls,
metal shades and oscillating fans,
your hospital bed, a chrome-sided throne,
reigns silent and still.

*The order of things*

You die the next day before
light troops the morning colors
or the baton of a birdsong choir
lifts to your transcendence,
miles from memory of bed,
home, and blue hydrangeas
choked by stagnant water.

In a quiet moment as I wipe
your lips the last time, you said,
*'tell Mom, I'll be by the North Star.'*

Like dust swirling to movement,
you travel home.

*The order of things*

**self-portrait underwater**

blame it on the moon, the songs my sister sings
wake the living with submerged thoughts,
phantasms we wring from tanks and shorts
puddle black at our sandy feet

memories of Rock Islands pile
like kukui nuts pushed at high tide,
sunlight waves through stringy kelp
my blonde hair streams surface-bound
mortal moorings undone
your hand pulls me, sister,
long knives glint metallic smiles
clenched between our teeth

armed mermaids, we float currents
unafraid, poison-tipped lionfish
and flapping manta rays fly above,
laughing jawed eels bob
beneath a Japanese Zero
nose down in anemoned ardor
feeding on forgotten emperors

we glide with seahorses
on watery hooves
galloping tiny, silent strides,
a swirling curtain jerks open,
green jack tails flash sequined scales,
starfish scatter a Milky Way
rainbow at coral's edge

## *The order of things*

a brown-spotted ray
splashes warnings in shallows,
death tangles in mangroves
across the lagoon,
faces swirl at the surface
calling our muffled names

let's stay here, sister,
where moon pushes our cradle
and warm liquid salt
loves a dangerous girl
swallows her whole
grit for an oyster tongue
too beautiful for air

*The order of things*

**Kitchen Vigil**

Stone-black river rushes beyond her window, birdsong forgotten on the muck-soft shore. Naked branches, trees with splayed roots, sediment of seasons sail past ocean-bound. In Mother's house of teaspoon-clattering-in-oatmeal bowl, cradled-cup-of-Folgers, fingers-puzzled-stiffly-into-place, palmed morning pills line yellow placemat, white cloth napkins wait-for-anyone. In her eyes, blue drains to milky water as my brother and I lift on both sides, a shadow-skin heavy with years. She lights at stories of music from an Austrian band, a polka with my father, laughs at the apple-pie-visit from the grandkids, shows us juice bottles in the refrigerator, the chili in Tupperware, teas in the cupboard. She imagines the great granddaughter who will come in the spring, now pear-sized and growing *quick as a wink*. Strawberry-blonde like me, she says, who will love sleep and bed as her grandmother, like we all do in long dreams without names. If stars share God's secrets, let them whisper to heads at both ends of this river. Blood and bone communion spill into the delta.

*The order of things*

**Drinking Tea in San Francisco**

I dream of a Japanese tea garden
where I search for my father's WW2 soldier-ghost
among Shinto spirits and Zen gardens raked like ocean waves.

On pebbled paths the kami laugh at their tricks
among screaming middle-schoolers on a scavenger hunt.
Busloads of slow-footed senior citizens block the way.

A monument stands to master-gardener Hagiwara,
a bronze-rusted lantern given by children to mark
a message of peace amidst wartime internment.

I drink genmaicha tea in bamboo shade.
Brown rice bobs at cup's bottom.
*You will meet someone important*, paper fortune curls.

I find memories of my father's soldier-ghost
in the eyes of the wrinkle-faced
woman, pouring tea, serving *arare*.

My father gentles now, his hand buried
deep in a tin box lined with medals
and Pacific nightmares.

*The order of things*

**Mirror, Flughafen Frankfurt, After a Bombing**

sister in the bathroom mirror
your hazel eyes are lighter than mine
your hair dark

heads uncovered
we re-twist ponytails   smooth lotion up to our elbows

you squeeze jasmine-scent from a white tube
me   ginger-cardamom from teal
we brush our teeth

spit at a drain   rinse with minty-green
mouthwash

moisturize faces   conceal dark circles
apply tinted balm to parted lips
with luggage packed

we look again   adjust
a navy hijab

a brown-brimmed hat
inhale long   heroic breaths
step toward trauma

disorienting flights

*The order of things*

**Presence**

Like in a dream I don't know how we arrive
standing on tree roots and broken bricks outside
a haunted Greek Revival, our shoulders touching.
Dear sister, you turn toward the school where children spill
each afternoon into the park beneath the moss-draped
oak, their simple games a torment for an imprisoned child
in starched petticoats across the street. You want to look.
Instead you drown in this night's unknown,
leached from catacombs, struggle against its current,
your phone flashing like a submerged beacon. On dream-wings
we fly to a dark room above rooftops, screened streetlight.
I don't know what I believe, except in the simplicity
of your warmth stretched next to me,
your breath mingled softly in my hair, your long kiss light
against my temple. A moment strung like a pearl
across the hollow of this separate-bodied life. Want
of a ghost girl beyond the shadows invites us to believe.

*The order of things*

**Sweet Dills**

Decay curls around your outbuildings like a wild thing claiming the yard. It squats near the hedges beneath afternoon sun. Weeds grow, metal rusts. Old plows and tractors salvaged for parts pile like corpses. The house withers before its joints give beneath a sway-backed roof. Vacancy, except for a dozen Mason jars glistening in the window of the summer kitchen. Three neat rows packed tight with smooth-skinned pickles, dill heads bursting like fireworks against the glass. The artistry of your skilled hands passes from your mother, her mother. Beautiful beyond blight. Your husband passes quietly in his Laz-y-Boy. A month later, flames consume it all. A backhoe buried what you couldn't. God knows the order of things. Earth, seed, rain and heat.

## *The order of things*

**Sheltering,**

they say, *pretend as if you have it*, and we do in shifts.

First, I choke on phlegm in my throat,
taste your hair as you lean listening
to my chest, back of your hand to my forehead
checking for fever. You bring me Tylenol.

Your face darkens in afternoon shadow.

Next, I imagine you balled beneath the quilt,
frayed-edge family totem against contagion.
You shiver like you did that Christmas in the ICU
when I thought you were lost to a dark dream.

We imagine touching, opening family memories:

see the Polaroid faces of the ponytailed girls, eating
cake, silly-tongued grins, shooting hoops in the drive?
Our son buys a gold-edged goblet from a flea market
for us, his guileless, six-year-old eyes, the real gift.

We find a letter written twenty-five years ago

in tidy scrawl to our oldest son's future self,
what would he do, where would he live? Who
would tell him isolation would be
his wishing star, a nation's hope, a global cure?

Later, we walk arm in arm across the hillside

sinking into earth's spongy warming while meadowlark's
pond-song ushers first peepers' grind. We touch
the bark of the river birch curled like tiny scrolls,
branches waving overhead thick with buds, proclaiming,

*haven't we survived this much, rooted to a solitary place?*

## *The order of things*

**May Vining**
   *for my son on his wedding day*

In Iowa, it's the month the Charlie starts to creep
and the earth writes wet fragrant poems
about the eternal newness of all things,
   the promise you can count on
   like fresh leaves at brittle ends.

My peony blooms on your birthday in May,
from roots not as old as you, not as loved as you,
but brilliant in its coming on, like a child unfolding
   from buds invisible
   until sunshine says

*this is the day.*

A mother cannot make her heavy heart
fly with bittersweet tears.

She can spread her memories in photos
across the lawn, point to her favorites,
laugh with you and your lover,
   but she cannot plant words
   wise and beautiful enough
   to nourish a hungry vine.

Today you are more than an eye-locked promise,

you are roots pushing into fresh dirt
twin cuttings   buds beneath a loving sun

   near flowers where
   butterflies and hummingbirds

wait to be born.

**Additional Acknowledgments**

Special thanks to the editors at the *Raw Art Review* for recognizing "Songs from the Summer Kitchen" as an honorable mention in its Charles Bukowski Prize for Poetry contest.

Gratitude to my community of Iowa poets who provide open, loving support and opportunity. Thank you to poets, writers and friends from Omega, Barnes and Noble Writers, and the Iowa Poetry Association. A special thanks to Dennis Maulsby, Marilyn Baszczynski, Julie Johnson, Jerry Narland, Steve Rose, and Shelly Reed Thiemen. A special thanks, too, for the amazing network of poets I continue to meet and who help me grow in the craft, including Rachel Marie Patterson and Dara-Lyn Shrager.

A heartfelt thank you Dara-Lyn Shrager, whose beautiful spirit and wise hand guided this project from beginning to end. I am blessed to call you editor and friend.

Thank you to friends and colleagues who have inspired and provided feedback. A loving thank you to my family for always being present despite the miles. And to my husband, John—thank you for encouraging this craziness, from the beginning of the journey to this place in the road. All my love.

www.ingramcontent.com/pod-product-compliance
Lightning Source LLC
LaVergne TN
LVHW041557070426
835507LV00011B/1142